PERSONAL

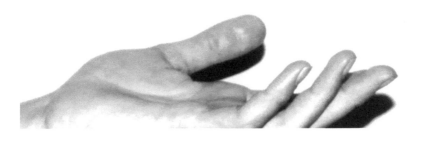

To Hamdi

AND THE REST

PERSONAL THINGS
AND
THE REST

Edin Suljic

Hafan Books

Hafan Books

c/o Tom Cheesman
Swansea University
Wales SA2 8PP UK

lulu.com/hafan   t.cheesman@swansea.ac.uk

All proceeds go to the charity
Swansea Asylum Seekers Support

Printed by Lulu.com in 2018

ISBN 9780995496675

(Dis)Contents

I've washed away the day with long sips of good coffee and said to myself: everything you've done, you've done well.

Howls, Shouts and Screams

On Love and Tribes in a New World Order

Some time ago I visited a part of the world that I once could loosely call 'my country'.

What was once one country is now seven.

If this sounds like a riddle – it is.

I use the word 'loosely' retrospectively because some people, like me, rightly or wrongly, once regarded that part of the world as their country, while for other people from the same part of the world, it was never wholly their country. Maybe they acknowledged only one part of it as their real or true or desired country.

So, when I go there now I tread carefully. After all, maybe you can't call some part of the world your own just because you were once told it was yours, or just because you once scaled its mountains, or swam in its seas, and covered its great distances by the night train. Nor can you make a claim on the cities of that country where you once whispered words of love. But apparently, I am told, you can claim cities that you have conquered with fire and destruction; any city. And I do wonder if one should only claim as one's country that small piece of land on which one stands, when the rest of the land starts breaking off and drifting away.

There, in that part of the world that I visited some time ago, I saw forests, mountains, blue sky and a lake. All of this was old and seemingly in its correct place, in peace with itself and with everything else. There I was, in this country, whose inhabitants had once been told to love each other for whatever reason. However, those people know from long experience that love is much more difficult to cultivate than hatred.

Love requires one to exist alongside others. Love cannot exist when one is alone. Love requires mutual respect and equality. It requires that the stronger support the weak and the healthier look after the sick. That type of love kind of exists in a family and extends to a tribe, as bonds are formed out of necessity and kinship. Even though such love has its price and sacrifices are always asked for in exchange. But here, inhabitants of this country have been asked to extend their love beyond their tribes. But these tribes carry their divisions and hold on to hurt from past injustices.

To practice love is the highest task among the duties of being a human. Despite this, even our spiritual and religious teachings often find a way to justify 'non-love'. Hence, inevitably, hatred prevails and conflicts arise, as it happened in my country. From the conflict, winners and losers emerge – each in a world of their own.

They are all blinded by refusing to see the consequences of their own actions; with their hearts dulled by ignoring the pain of others. But the hate, per se, is not a good enough reason to exist. Once the enemy is defeated there is no-one left to hate and so inevitably the winners and losers reach out to each other with some kind of love offerings. Love also with a price tag.

There, in that part of the world, which was once my country, I came across scores of professional dealers of all sorts: manipulators, missionaries, mercenaries, adventurers, chancers, drop outs of all kinds and occasional idealists; all of them promoters of imported love.

In a blind, dualist world of love and hate, good and bad, a kind of fictional world of good is created, through all types of bad actions. All that rhetoric belongs to yet another tribe, a tribe which is stronger than those native tribes. In fact, this tribe is strongest of them all. Equipped with modern mythology and legends, they make claims on history, science and progress, claiming that they will 'better the world'. 'After all', they say, 'see how good it is now, for humanity today, where we have arrived. It was never better'.

For some, indeed it is better. For a few – much better.

And those few intend to keep things just as they are.

But back to this country of mine. As after any conflict, some things got better. The winners, as always, claim that their win is due to their superior strength and unity, and that the fight was for a just cause. The victory is never thought to be due to the fact that they have taken something from those who have lost. And the losers are left to count their losses – and to fend for themselves. That is the space into which the visitors' entourage moves in. The strongest always look for the new recruits to further strengthen their power. Just as the brutal looked for slaves to increase their wealth.

And then there are the servants of God who seek wounded souls, to heal them. In that part of the world, which was once my country, those in the Service of God were always present. Domini Cani – Dogs of God. Those who would, apart from establishing temples, when required, reset a human soul for a substantial fee.

If the strongest and the winners set the moral compass, then what is left for the defeated and the losers? If the party line, or a letter from a scripture is all that is needed for a good life, is there any place for doubters and defectors?

What are the weak to do when help comes in the form of one or another temple? When the word gets around that help comes as a result of becoming pious, is assigning oneself to some kind of new-old tribe the way forward, even if that really means a deeper separation between the winners and losers?

Almost every prominent hill in the region around the town where I was born is now occupied by a newly built mosque or church. After all, weren't we all born just to be put to some kind of use? But, by whom?

And seemingly, the way to a good life quickly becomes apparent.

We all believe in the same things and everything will be well. Right?

Except, the world today, apparently, functions on the principles of democracy. We choose our representative and our representative will have our best interest at heart. Except, when the new-old tribes' parties are formed as nationalist parties. Then put rich and poor into the mix and you soon find out that being involved in politics and keeping the nationalist divisions alive is a sure way of keeping oneself in a job.

And where in all of this is there space for creativity, and for the artists who are compelled to ask questions?

In my hometown, the mayor is a published writer. Amongst his duties, he takes part in running an annual literary festival where the best writing from the region is celebrated. This is a region of once warring tribes, who speak shades of the same language.

On the face of it, it's great to have a writer to run a town; but on the flip side, the entire region is in economical meltdown and cultural downturn. Like everywhere else, reality TV and minor celebrities shape the aspirations of the younger generation. Reality TV and minor celebrities are powerful tools in the hands of the aforementioned entourage. At the same time nationalist politicians need a cultural milieu around them. So, paradoxically, the position of certain accomplished artists is as good as it can be.

Film festivals pop up regularly, and celebrities of all kinds turn up at them. But art as a powerful social force is in decline, with struggling galleries and theatres. Does this sound familiar? Isn't that how a strong, modern society functions? Or is that a privilege of strong, victorious societies?

At the same time, strong societies, societies that have achieved their strength by brutality, can afford to have 'free speech', critical thinking, provocative art, even experimenting with new models of society, that 'need to be tested somewhere else first'.

And what about weak, fractured societies like those that emerged from what was once my country?

Art has always offered what institutionalized religions and politics can't – inspiration and honesty, respectively – but art was never enough to sustain life itself.

So freedom of speech, censorship, and provocative art are all part of the means by which a society finds its strength, finds a way to exist in a world where the strong crush the small as a way of self-preservation.

So, what do you get when you 'Balkanise' one big, functioning country?

You might get one, now smaller, still strong country, but you will certainly also get several weak countries and they will be prime territories for the foreign entourage, for the army of chancers, and the Dogs of God. And so the strong and victorious will continue using their strange moral compass to embark on a recruitment process. Imported fake love keeps sowing seeds of hate.

I sometimes wonder if the people of that land that was once my country will ever be able to live together again like they did in that mythical, legendary nation. Whenever I see those forests, mountains and lakes, I think it is still possible. Good people grow from that land. Love is the best medicine to follow hate. But I also wonder if that love I mentioned is really the privilege of just one family, or one tribe. The strongest.

This essay was presented at the conference 'Danger of Words in the Age of Danger' organized by Exiled Writers Ink at SOAS in 2017.

I've trimmed dried parts of the leaves on my plants, and wondered why in stories there are always some troubled, innocent souls who have to die.

Brothers

When you said that I should leave the house and find my
own, I said nothing and left...
because you are my brother.
And I went away and built my own house,
you came and planted a tree...
because you are my brother.
And then we dug a well, drew water and drank it from each
others' hands. And then you helped me cultivate a garden.
And then I grew corn and made bread from it
and we ate the bread...
because you are my brother.

And when the great fire burnt my house down you came
round with bread and you helped me build a new house...
because you are my brother.

Next time you came round, you came with some strange
men and you told me that we don't speak the same language
any more.
I said you are my brother and I learnt my language from
you.
But you let those men take my wife and my children from
me.
And you said nothing to the men.
But you are my brother.
And then you let the men destroy my garden and fill my
well up and leave me for dead. And you said nothing.
But you are my brother.

And I was dead for a long time.
And then I learned to live again. And then I came to your house and asked for some water. And you said nothing.
But you are my brother.
And you went on to build a tall wall around your house and let the men throw stones at me. And you said nothing.
But you are my brother.
And I grew weaker and weaker left alone in the desert of life.
And you did nothing.
But you are my brother.

And then the great flood came and tore away the walls and your house. And I drank a new life from the waters of the flood.
And I grew stronger and stronger. And I went to look for you. Because you are my brother.
And I found you. You were old and weak. Your men had left you. And I thought about leaving you to die. But I didn't.
I looked at you and I saw myself.
Because you are my brother.

And I helped you learn to live again. And you looked at me and said that I looked just like you.
And I said I am your brother.
And we went on and build a new house and dug a new well.
And we drew water and drank it from each others' hands...
because we are brothers.
And then we cultivated a new garden. And then we grew corn and made bread from it and we ate the bread...
because we are brothers.

2011/2016

Gooseberry Pickers

They come silent, on their tiptoes, with amplified heartbeat
Some good, some bad, all without a chance to prove either
They smile as their eyes search for something familiar
With their tongues tied,
Those who passionately argued that justice lives on these shores,
Those who talked of every forbidden fruit on offer
And those who blamed their forefathers for their bad luck;
They have all left their fields behind.
Here – the tale is told –
You only need to bend down to pick up money.

And they carefully place the fruits in baskets,
arranging them (almost) with love and affection,
with the intention of those who befriend every stone
in search of their lost hearts
and with the serenity of those who have found peace of
mind at last – as each new layer brings them closer to their
hopes,
and their hopes are their crimes – hopes for a better life.

They couldn't know that our summer puddings taste sour,
even with piles of caster sugar, and yet, no one has ever
dared to make them without gooseberries.
They all looked upon this kingdom as the holiest of them all,
where everything is considered a sin
Yet, new sins multiply day-by-day,
and the worst sin of all is speaking the truth
As truth is a pudding that no one has ever made sweet.

They comfort themselves by humming
tunes from their forgotten lands
as their tears mix with soap in their washing bowls.

Author's note
I have been told by those who have been fruit picking with gypsies:
"You definitely don't mess about picking them carefully, you're paid
by the weight of what you pick – so you just chuck everything in…
stones, leaves, unripe fruit, etc. Have you ever seen fruit pickers
working? It's not a sedate, quiet action – they frantically scrabble
around snatching at fruit."
My fruit pickers are not of this kind.

The Way We Have Approached the Book of Changes

For the Chinese cockle pickers who drowned
in Morecombe Bay on February 4th 2004

When the great King Wen had thrown his yarrow sticks for
the last time, he stayed silent for several centuries.

Then he said:

*There will be a time that is no different from any other time; a time
when inferior men will rule men of virtue, when those who are
willing to hold up heaven will preserve the possibility for change;
the possibility that gives hope to humankind.*

*That is a task that no man can endure, except those who live as if
they are not alive.*

*In times like these heaven merges with soil and water to produce
new sons.*

*And the sons of the sons of my sons will live to die in the arms of
foreign women who will whisper...*

"The Atlantic is the beast my love..."

Orange

On the destruction of orange groves
in the Gaza Strip, May 2003

You can know the number of segments of an orange
                              – without peeling it.
Such is the art of perfection.

Oranges are striving for perfection.

Under the skin of an orange is the Universe.
Every drop of rain,
every song of every bird that ever rested
on the branches of an orange tree
                              – remembered.

You can't know what is under the skull of a man.
Man is lost in his own chaos.

A brute that fails to look upon the stars through
the orange blossom remembers nothing
and is of no use to anyone.

Tattoo

A curse for an arms dealer

Tattoo me with something that will make me beautiful,
But...
Tattoo me with something that will draw out pools of
blood...
For blood is what I seek.
For my soul is just an empty shell and I am not I until
I prove myself in cries of others.
Not the cries of admiration...

Tattoo me with MOAB and symbol 155MM

For my soul is a shell filled with explosive.

Curtain Call

On tragic events in Dubrovka Theatre
in Moscow in October 2002

There, you see,
                nothing is real
A house of illusions
A safe place to be

Tired,
Gods rest there.
Brute and Gentle live there.
Every dream begins and ends there.

There, you see,
                it is possible to learn to cry
For real,
Laughter, laughter, laughter...

You see, there will be no applause tonight,
Nor ever again.

Give me back my smiles
My tears
Maskva ne poverit slezam
(Moscow won't trust tears).

Beneath the Mountain

For the miners in Turkey, 2015

My uncle. He was a miner. Returning home black as Guinness. Home he'd built for himself.

My neighbour. He was a miner. Returning home with a handful of liquorice. Home he'd built for himself.

My other uncle. He was a miner. Returning home with a bagful of dominoes. Home he'd built for himself.

My other neighbour. He was a miner. Returning home black as a coffee. Home he'd built for himself.

My third neighbour. He was a miner. Returning home with pockets full of marbles. Marbles flashing in the sunlight. Home he'd built for himself.

My third uncle, who was a miner, he said to me: "But you don't have a home of your own – and even a doggy has a home."

My third uncle. He died in his home. Home he'd built for himself.

And my second uncle.   And my first uncle.
And my neighbour.   And my other neighbour.
And my third neighbour.

My father. He was a miner. He didn't return home.
Home he'd built for himself.
And for me.

The Years of Living Silently

The Quivering of a Window-Pane
Waiting for Transformation

The window-pane in my room is greeting you.
With its bright eye of a neighbour's light
With its open green arms grown out of terracotta
With its heart of a lit candle in a blue glass
With its desire to become twilight blue mountains
in which it is reflected.

(Shall we ever know what is the longing
of a window-pane
waiting to become a landscape ?)

Letter to Friends

A letter is timeless.
It contains the moment in which it is written
and the moment in which it is read.
I am writing it now and you are reading it now.

Here, the rain.
There – imagine rain in any way you can.
Pools and pavements and umbrellas.
Morning, children, sea and cyclists, clouds and chimneys:
Wet.
Then rain dripping from roofs and the sound of
An accordion somewhere at the corner, under the eaves.
And a postlady and newspapers and everlasting drops
Under the street lights.
And water in a gutter and a window-pane
With countless signatures.

Then, rising over all, the huge and ruddy sun…

*

I could re-write one street or one day or one town.
Crocuses have flowered.
Here
halfway down my street
underneath huge plane trees in the courtyard of one of those
common buildings with flats for ordinary people.
It is once more going to be spring.
There

I imagine myself as a clock which is counting eternity
in its mechanism.
Walking into the newspaper shop and buying a paper.
Greeting the shopkeeper.
Stopping by the flower shop. Buying flowers for my room.
Going to the greengrocer's for carrots, cabbage, leeks, millet
and beans. Exchanging smiles with the shop girl.
Sitting in a café and watching people passing by.
Listening to the waitress's dutiful kindness, knowing that I
like her.
"Yes," I say, "I am well again today."

Walking back home I remember that I haven't talked for a
while
with my friend in the bookshop on the corner,
and that I haven't seen my neighbour for some days.
And that long is the list of those dear to me whom
I am no longer able to greet.

How a Letter Comes to Be

Bright, washed and wet afternoon is rising from the rainy
morning
And I am writing a letter.
Someone will need to open the envelope.
Like opening a trunk or a room or a window or the sky.
Open the trunk.
Nothing happens.
The trunk full of quivering expectations in clear lines of space,
Still echoing the click of the key in the lock.
Open the room.
Again, nothing happens.
The room full of walls and scattered splashes of light on the floor
And echoes of unspoken words.
Open the window.
The window drawn by the roofs of neighbouring houses
Thick with antennas,
And involved in the life rolling down the street below.
Yet everything steps back with gentleness,
Allowing the gaze to multiply itself in a haze on the horizon,
There,
Where the sky opens.
The sky opens by a flight of birds. And by rain.
By clouds moving aside. By the arc of a rainbow.
By shooting stars.
And the letter … the letter is opened by
Dear …
Like the trunk, the room, the window, the sky.
Like treasure, like magic.
Explored with a fluttering heart and shining eyes.
That is how a letter comes to be.

Morning Prayer

Oh God, what a miracle that we are still alive today.

Nobody takes it seriously any more.
Nobody's eyes are wide open any more.
And nobody is pinching himself
          to check if it is really him,
if everything is exactly like he left it yesterday:
Everything is here, yet it is not a dream.

Nobody is enchanted any more
          with the pulse of life in us,
carried by childish curiosity
and innocently devoted
to life's unfolding as such.

As if every new morning is everybody's right.

Rose-Colossi

Rain drops are signing themselves in a morning picture
framed by the window-pane of my room,
making the colours run.

How do the roses feel under this wet sky?
Here I am, standing naked in the rain,
naked under the sky which itself is falling headlong.
And water is flowing over my skin just as it flows over
the roses spiralling towards their wombs.

In the joy of my own nothingness,
I am holding this cruel heaven together with rose-colossi.

Personal Things

Note on the Rose

With N.A.

The question was:
What is the Being of a rosebud's heartbeat?
The insight of the one who was and hence knows he is:
If the rosebud is cherished long enough close to the heart
(in the inside pocket of a coat, for instance)
the two hearts become one.
The Question is the Answer:
Is there a God?
Or: Is love everything?
Or …

The world should be seen through the eyes of Dying Lovers.

How Things Were Before They Got Rough

I am wrapping myself with your scarf and I am walking out
    into the day
        into the light
        into life
with the scarf that once belonged to your father.
I am taking away your chance to write a song about the scarf.

At the end of a street a solitary tree is waiting for me.
I will wrap your scarf around it and I will walk through the
town, weak and kind as if after a drunken night
when the wine is still flowing through my veins.

You see, you are the things I am made of.
You see, things are hard nowadays.
Things are rough. That is why I am calling you.
You are helping me to learn to live in this way.

You remember the time when the eyes of all of us
Became wide open?
When each of us merged into the other,
when everyone became everyone for everyone.
You see, I was missing those things.
I was dying without them.
That is why I was calling you.
Now, you see, I've learned to live with those rough things.
Now we are multiplying ourselves in everything we meet
or touch in passing.
You see, we are wrapping them in us.
You see, we will not lose us.

How to Make a Pot of Tea

She asked me if I have any talents.
I could write a poem, I said.

And I remember a quartette of teapots
softened by tea through time,
looking at us from the shelf, benevolently,
like drunks, jovial at their very own private party,
seeing the world with the eyes of those who have seen
everything.

I remember
Jacques Prévert's "How to Paint the Portrait of a Bird".

And I remember that it was necessary to confirm my
existence each new morning by getting used to every new
day as the retina of the eye adapts to the light (recognising a
day by slow, soft movements of the hands which were
drawing themselves in the air), by sleepy faces and locks of
hair in which dreams still swarm (as, aha, there you are, here
in front of me and I love you again today), by the
comfortable warmth of the porcelain in which life fades
away with each sip.

And I remember that it was necessary to live all these lives.
And that is how I've learned how to make a pot of tea.

Recognising

on the train, during a journey through Terra
Incognita, from Pula to Neoplanta, with S.C.
— The train has stopped…

Voice 1	What is the name of this place?
Voice 2	The Vineyards of Karlovac.
Voice 1	Imagine information in my passport: Address – The Vineyards of Karlovac, Name – Istrian Peach. And you, where do you live?
Voice 2	Oh, just Up and Above, Beyond the Clouds, in Port of Roses.
Voice 1	And who are you?
Voice 2	I am Bird.
Voice 1	I always thought you were Droplet?
Voice 2	Yes, sometimes I am Droplet. Droplet which washes flowers of Istrian Peach.
Voice 1	That is how Droplet becomes Fruit.
Voice 2	Yes, though this time I am Bird.
Voice 1	So you can land on the branches of Istrian Peach and build a nest. (Then it is a common nest for Bird and Peach.)*
Voice 2	That is how Fruit becomes Bird and you can take off to Beyond the Clouds.
Voice 1	You mean to Port of Roses, Beyond the Clouds, just Up and Above the Vineyards of Karlovac?
Voice 2	Yes.

*(the thought of an observer)

Sometimes I dream about the war in which I've never been.
Then I wake up and cry for all who died in that war.

Terra Incognita

I step barefoot on a scorching rock
and stand there until I grow into it.
I look up at the sky veiled by the mist of July's heat
and gaze at the sun's globe until my eyes water with tears.
Then I spread my arms
    open my hands
    take off and fall.
I rise, cover the scorched earth with kisses, say my prayer.
And then everything begins anew.

The War of the Roses

Once I had a garden of roses.
I used to celebrate their smell and worship their forms.
Many passers-by would stop on their way and bend their
heads to their beauty, until one night a rock-slide destroyed
my garden, mashing rose petals with the soil.

On the ruins of their smells I built again the garden
and enclosed it with a wall.
Passers-by said:
We will help you build a taller and stronger wall.
And they built it. And they set night-watches to protect my
garden from the rocks, and other misfortunes.
Now many more strangers were coming from everywhere
to offer admiration to this Kingdom of Beauty.
We want to look after them too, they said to the night-
watchers.
We want to be close to them and to drink from their petals.
No, said the night-watchers, we are the only keepers of the
Beauty.
And the others said: They belong to us as much as to you.
Why are you hiding them from us?

That is how the war of the roses started.
In anger and hatred they destroyed my garden.
So I began to cultivate the garden in myself,
the garden of the imprinted smells and colours of my roses.
Since then,
I've met many others with gardens inside themselves.

Death of a Friend

a dream

I've known heroes
who have, without fear, dived into
      the darkest whirlpools.
Shoals of silence would move aside with respect,
to give way to their lithe, spindle-shaped bodies.
I was always afraid.
I owe my courage to them. I own only my fears.

I've dreamt of quivering willows,
delighted by the movements of the water,
stretched into greeting hands from platforms,
      rooted in the eternal desire for travel.
      In love with the forever-leaving waves
they wrap them with an armour-shirt woven with their own
fabric.
      The same willows
      which have suckled me with juices,
      which dammed by the bark rise into the sky.
        Without them
        the river of my own blood would dry up
        in perpetual sinking into itself.

Assassins

They follow my every step. They know me well.
All my mistakes, all the things I loved.
They know all my secret shortcuts.
They turn up at the right corner long before I get there.
And I don't try to run away.
How could I? After all, I too, know them well.
I fed them. I got drunk with them night after night.
We sat around a table. I looked at their eyes.
I held their hands. Some I kissed.
Many I held in my embrace.
And I betrayed them, many a time.

So I wait, knowing they are waiting.
I hope they will come out of the shadows.
But they don't. They won't come closer.
They wouldn't let me smell their perfume
or inhale a wisp of their cigarettes' smoke.
Like this, we remain forever locked in; they,
who never leave me, I, who never let go of them.

Most of all I fear you, my love.
You know every hollow under my skin.
You know when I breathe out.
You could stop my heart with one touch... But you don't...
You just lie there at night, next to me, under our blanket,
encircling every bend of my body.
There we remain forever in waiting.
I, who am waiting for your kiss, for a blow,
and you, who are waiting for my hope to fade away.
But the blow doesn't come and the hope doesn't fade.

Last Sunday I saw the flower which I remember from my grandmother's garden. And I was happy that day.

Before Me

Here... Hear... Let me tell you a story.
Maybe a dream...
And if it is my dream, then it is my story, too.

There were three of them, and they were supposed to tell me, one by one, something they had never told me before, like a confession, and I was hoping to hear the words I had wanted to hear all my life... And I was supposed to say something gentle in return, something that would make them as fragile as a crumbling crust of bread, or like an old love letter that falls to pieces between fingers when it is touched. And then we sat down together besides low tables, shoulder to shoulder, and laughter and the rhythm of conversations reverberated around us like some kind of strange dance of all the things unseen. And there were bottles of wine opened and the sound of clinking glasses seemed like crickets in the fields, and then from somewhere came a song as if brought by the wind; a female voice, low and high at the same time; a voice that seemed to stir the blades of grass, and to lift the smells of summer into the air, and then I knew that I was sitting between my mother and my father, the three of us, together for the first time, just before I would be born.

2011

Autumn Breath

morning, late September 1992

Everything smells of autumn. And it's summer.
I sense a familiar taste in my mouth.
As if I were about to be born.
As if I could taste my mother's milk.

I recall heavy morning dews
and the sun's rays in a cobweb
woven among almost dry corn leaves.
The sound of the waking clock.

Childhood scenes stirred.
Alive like a breath.
Spacious like the inside of my skull.
A boy who is a man.
A man grown enough to carry himself, a boy,
on his shoulders.
And the picture of my mother,
Incarnation of Love.

And what is left when the magic stops?
One more tattoo on the soul?

Dress Rehearsal

Every night when I close my eyes,
Before sleep comes upon me
I choose the costume in which I am going to die
From an open trunk...

And then in sleep, I play my heroes.
Countless destinies, yet in each of them, I look for myself.

When the scenery of the night fades
And the first patches of a pale new day start to appear,
Tired,
I close the trunk and wake up,
Hoping that the coming night I will choose well.

A Poet of the New World

The Key to a Friend's House

A Gypsy woman asked me once
– Finding a key on the road – what would I do.

I would leave it there – I replied.

So, you'd pass by the friendship, she said.

The key to a friend's house is in your hands
– Wherever you go.
Don't knock – just let yourself in.
It is the house you'll feel welcomed in.
The house where you can rest while doing
Whatever you need to do.
The house you'll be safe in.
You'll be leaving all your fears upon entering.

The Key to a Friend's House is on the Road
– Just pick it up.

New York, spring 2015

A Word in Your Ear

Everything ends washed up on these docks.
The scum,
And the specks of gold.

Thou, who art here,
Brought by the currents of life that swirl and twist
In unbeknown ways to Thee-and-me,

Don't curse Thy bad luck.

For Thou hast been piled up here with dried seaweed
To slowly wilt
As newly hatched seagulls' chicks come to feed.

But,
A word in Thine Ear –
'Tis her name you want to hear –
Barbara.
The sound which makes everyone dash –
For one more pint.
And by the last orders' hour,
Thou wilt not cry out any more
For being thrown onto this shore.

Ear In, Spring Street, Established 1817. New York, spring 2014

Saturdays' Predictions

Like taking a wrong turn on his way home,
he often felt as if he'd made the wrong choice
at a life-defining crossroads,
and although he would, eventually, get to his home,
he would feel as if it was some other home –
not the one he was supposed to find on his return
if he had made a different choice.

The life he lived in the end
wasn't the one he was hoping for,
nor the one he would have chosen
if it was described to him.

Still, like when he was writing his predictions
for the teams that had all the odds to loose,
he followed his heart, hoping that
one day it would be different –
that the life he wanted for himself
would be the one he was living.

After all, one has to make choices:
one for a home win, *zero* for a draw, and
two for an away win – only a dozen or so guesses.
But the minnows hardly ever tasted victory,
no matter how hard he wanted them to win –
and the big guys always got what they aimed for
one way or another, even if they kept
knocking each other every so often along the way.

Occasionally, he would think: what

if he had made a different choice
in which he would be living that other life
where he was behind the team that
kept winning week after week...

Instead, he would rearrange his disappointments
until the following Saturday
when he would again write down his predictions,
on which he never placed bets.

St James Gate, New York City, 2015

How to Stop Dizziness

Here, even the poets kill each other
        – for an inspiration.
But poets are kind souls and death by the hand of a poet

is an easy death.

Still, Les Enfants du Paradis live somewhere else.
The tired old universe would stop cranking but for those
who propel it further, as their vision is unperturbed.

Once being set off, the carousel is mesmerising,
yet its motion depends on those whose chests puff
and who choke on tears.
Still, The Children of Paradise live somewhere else.

For a few of those who manage to get off,
the spinning continues for a while.

The best way to stop dizziness is to watch one's step.

Step, breath, step, breath, cobble stone, step...

There are plenty of cobble stones here
for when the time of change comes.

Be careful my child, the mob is always there, ready to cheer.

Boston, Somerville, 2013

Shakespeare on the Run
and
the New Patriotism

Bards Without Borders

In 2015 I visited my old homeland of former Yugoslavia for six weeks, which was the longest time I'd spent there since I left before the war in 1991. My stay there coincided with the height of unprecedented mass migration of people through Europe. The bulk of them passed through the territories of former Yugoslavia. Day after day there was news about thousands of people in an unending human chain going through Macedonia then Serbia then Croatia and finally Slovenia, their last exit gate before entering into the Promised Land of affluent Europe. Various barriers started appearing on the borders of that promised land, as well as various responses towards those people.

The absurdity of the whole situation affected me profoundly. Les than 25 years ago, people of those newly formed countries of the former Yugoslavian republics were affected by the war, people from Bosnia and Croatia were on the run with their belongings bundled up in plastic bags or suitcases, and now they themselves were watching other unfortunate humans running away from wars or just walking along with an aim to get better life somewhere else (which I believe is everybody's right anyhow).

I didn't experience the Yugoslavian war directly. I went away just in time. My closest family and friends remained.

We who are fortunate to live away from such disasters can't comprehend the experiences of those who are personally affected. The news we get is filtered, polished, manipulated, trickled to us, so it doesn't disturb us much as we go about our daily business. That's how the news about the war in Yugoslavia came through to us, 25 years ago and that's the way the news about any other war is presented now. But the relentless presence of misery, tragedy, suffering on one's doorstep is a completely different experience.

On my return to London I began working with a collective of poets of refugee and migrant origins, *Bards Without Borders*. It was 400 years after Shakespeare's death. Shakespeare was able to write about any amount of gore and guts being spilled, murders committed, eyes gouged out. I portrayed him as someone who has been broken by the real tragedies of our times; as My Mate, whose words show humanity's frailties, weaknesses, and cruelty; the suffering we inflict on each other; but whose work and legacy is an inspiration for generations of writers, and in turn their writing helps to bring awareness about the consequences of the actions of one part of the world towards another – the relationship between the weak and the strong.

My Mate Shakespeare

The first time I met Shakespeare, he looked nothing like
himself, nothing like that depiction of a poster boy with a
hipster beard one comes across every so often.
No, he was tall, scrawny, flamboyant, thin-moustached and
bespectacled, with large hands into which his guitar almost
disappeared as he sang, perched on a low stool, in the
theatre's green room, where we would occasionally be
allowed to sneak in, as aspiring writers and actors, to join
the post-press-night party.
In those days we shared many breakfasts, mainly coffee and
cigarettes, and sometimes a boiled egg given to us by a kind
cook in the theatre's canteen.
And our fortunes took many turns...
Some claimed his work as their own.
Some complained about too many foreigners in his plays
(As if we don't have our own trulls, they'd say).
Others even claimed he never wrote anything, or worse, that
he never existed.
My mate Shakespeare...
Every so often he'd ask me if I was still writing, then say:
– Keep writing, keep writing, mi duck...
But then, he ripped apart my first play.
That's too serious, boyo, he said, and inserted an innuendo
into every second speech.
He was madly in love with this blonde, petite, round-eyed
actress who was patiently waiting for her lucky break on
stage, and for him to come to her garret.
Almost addicted to bingo and drinking a lot of poor quality
brandy, he got himself into many troubles by attacking so

many kings, offending so many celebrities and ridiculing politicians; and he wrote too many plays about deformity and cross-dressing.

Even his small girlfriend turned out to be a man in disguise.

Then the war tore everything apart, and I haven't seen him since.

The world entered into this never-ending war.

I heard the stories… He married a very different girl and they had two beautiful children and they lived somewhere in the outskirts of the City.

He doesn't go to the theatre anymore.

But then, like most stories about him, these too, turned out to be unreliable. I saw him once more – in the East End.

That last time I saw him, he looked like a broken man. My friend. My indestructible friend.

Something or somebody managed to do it to him.

I suppressed a cry inside myself. What is left for the rest of us?

What will happen to us if people like him could be broken?

Then he leaned over his glass of cheap brandy and whispered

– Keep writing, keep writing, boyo…

Tell Me

Tell me, oh, why, why did you have to die,
Now, when everyone wants to celebrate your life?
You coward. You were my mate.
Leaving us to the likes of those
whose art is opposite to every good,
yet they speak of nothing but being just...
They're inventing a new world day after day,
A world in which no trace of their evil-doing is left.

Yes, I know, there were times when even I too forgot about
you as
joys and sorrows took over my life.

Soon the smell of wild garlic will fill up our woodlands and
St George's name will be on everyone's lips.
But I guess you don't care about wild garlic anymore.
You've been smelling it each spring for four hundred years.
You'd care for mandrake, right? There is no more mandrake
since they stopped hanging. There are no more real men
either.

Still, I'd like you to be here. They might slaughter a suckling
pig for your wake and there will be a barrel or two of golden
ale.
Yes, I know you don't care for ale, that's why
I smuggled a flask of your favourite brandy through
security.

I know it might be rather overwhelming for you to see so
many

wearing t-shirts bearing your visage, explaining to each other
what you really meant with one word or another.
Still, I'd like you to come to the party.
We'll sneak out onto the balcony and puff on counterfeit
foreign cigarettes, watching it all as if the world's a stage.

Now, they want to bury your words. In some kind of a
strange ritual. Apparently, they stand for something wrong.
How do they imagine doing it? As if your words weren't
their words? As if your words weren't part of themselves?
As if your words weren't for making wrongs turn into
rights?

You wouldn't believe it, but they've put all of you inside one
single, big black book, as if you were a churchman or a man
of law. A black box. As if there's something to be found in
there.

You were looking the world square in the eye and getting
responses, just as your words, played out on the stage,
would have sounded as a waterfall, as church bells, as a
battle cry, as a lover's whisper...

But I guess no man is the master of his life, let alone of his
death.

So, when you arrive, give me a gentle tap on the shoulder.
I might be dancing tango, or putting on a new costume, but
grab
a pint of that ale and don't get into any fights before I join
you.

Tell Me More, My Girl

You might be surprised, or you might just chuckle, knowing
that your name can't be uttered any more – nor your words.
Nowadays, there are agents listening at the corners for your
phrases spoken by us; they are sifting through our mail.

The very same phrases we were inventing
lying naked under our quilt, giggling –
resting on a milky coloured bosom,
uttering dirty jokes is almost a crime.

We speak a strange language and we are watched over.
And making a living from one's trade becomes harder and
harder.

It was easy then to work as a seamstress during the day,
turning rugs into costumes for the shows.
And at night, there's a lot more one can put under a girl's
skirt.
The whole universe. A stage. A play.
You won't find that sort of inspiration in a fine lady's
chambers
would you? Or so they say.

The Land. The Sea. The Ship. The Desert.

What is a Ship? Is it a House? Is it a Fish?
Is it a big Bowl dropped into the Sea?
None of the above and all of them, perhaps.
Why would you abandon the land for a metal cage set in the
middle of endless blue water?
The ship's guts smelling of oil and its ribcage filled up with
human hearts beating with hope for a better life.
Humans, clinging onto whatever is around until
only hope is left.
And while a ship moves humans are anchored by hope.

But, moving into the desert, across vast waters – for hope?
Must human life on Earth be an endless repetition of
Biblical mythology?
Who writes those stories?
Who spills this suffering like a child that spills a glass of
milk while carrying it across the smooth floor?
And where is this promised place of peace before death?
Where is that life before death? Why life, if all of it is an
endless stream of bloodshed and running away from terror?

We were in a Desert. And a bird fell from the Skies. A bird
you can't eat. A metal bird. An airplane.
But we made tools to eat with from its skeleton and wings.
And tools to dig into the sand.
And we grew life out of a Desert.
We came out of the hell of war and every new day was for
creating the world anew.
Given the peace we were able to turn dust and dew into
loaves of bread. We created palaces out of canvas. And feasts

out of scraps.
We created our Country, our flag, our anthem and we called it
New Life.

We are from an Empire that was so vast
its borders were falling off the world map – that's how big it
was. And I am carrying it all in here… In my chest… The
Whole Empire.
Everything was celebrated and nothing was favored.
Even less feared.
I am telling you. I am a cartographer and a flag maker.

Now I live on this Island and I struggle to find what is it that
has bound me here. My past loves? My children that I didn't
father?

And who placed this Island in the middle of the Sea to
anchor those human hopes by means of service?
Service to the Country, to the Ruler, to God?
Who chooses those employed in service and those
who are to be sacrificed?
Does running away from terror train humans in service?
Is terror born out of service?
Who amongst us is to do terror as service?
Is saying *yes* all that is needed to eliminate one's own terror
even if it means dealing with the terror of others forever after?
Is that loyalty?
Who do you assign yourself to?
To the strongest, as long as the strongest is winning?

Sons of this Island do not question the actions of their fathers.

On This Side of the Future

Here am I – in a timeless zone,
where there are no clocks, snitchers on time.
Just the tick-tock of human hearts –
and the live streaming of my future life.

I will be given a task to wash my hands thoroughly.
Such an act requires long and precise training.

First, grabbing a tiger by the tail by rinsing out one's soul
well.
Then ogling a picture of oneself for a long time,
a picture (that) remembers just a single instant.
The whole set of instructions for the future.

1994/2017

A Flag Maker and an Anthem Writer

Tell me, tell me again, how was it…
When your grandma asked you to put a thread
through the eye of a needle,
just as mine did…
Were you laughing?
Oh, granny…

The first time I met your father, he sized me up,
despite his glazed eyes, and said:
There'll be nearly a hundred inches to stitch for your suit.

And here are we, I am watching you struggle to put a thread
into your fancy sewing machine as you shout:
I see, said a blind man!

You who've spent an entire man's life
building a safe place to be –
an armour, out of something as fragile as fabric.

And life as such goes on…
We give each other what we can or what we must.
Your fingers keep getting sewn into a new suit and my
pencil keeps breaking under the weight of Heaven.

And we go on building this Country anew –
You're stitching its tattered flag and I'm spelling its anthem.

Night in Which I Know You

Tonight
My eyes are piercing through the millions of years to come
And when they meet yours I want to be in them.

Tonight
I travel to forgotten lands of all of my sojourns,
I walk through the cities of my youth, proud,
I am taking you with me.

Tonight
I celebrate broken strings for all the lost loves,
I stumble on stairways of fragile notes in an attempt
To walk through dreams.

I breathe the smell of vast space in your hair and each
Breath explodes in my chest into an eternal beginning.

Be gentle

You know

Tonight I am holding your heart on my palm.

Joe's Kid

for the people of Spitalfields and Whitechapel

And a skip and a hop amongst the piss and Halal
And a skip and a hop amongst the piety and the vice
Skip 'n' hop.
'Cause there on the corner is my heart
And when the sky opens, it's blue
Just like it always was where my heart is.

And a skip and a hop through the crowds and the punks
'Cause there on the corner is my heart
And when the leaves in the treetops speak
I listen like I always did where my heart is.

And a skip and a hop around a bandstand
Where the music is never played,
But I hear the song that my heart always sang.

And a skip and a hop by the flock of bathing birds
And the flapping of their wings
Takes me where my heart is.

And a skip and a hop by a bench
Where the lovers coo
And I know my love is where my heart is.
And a skip and a hop by the thugs and the hoods
And I know that my courage is where my heart is.

And a skip and a hop by the spot
Where my tears first fell
And my heart dried them off
And a skip and a hop and I know where I go
Skip 'n' hop
'Cause on the corner is my heart waiting for me.

The Scrapyard of Poetry

Kitchen Poem for All Seasons

(serve as much as you like)

Heroes get medals
And artificial limbs.
Admirals get monuments
And ever-lasting glory,
For which three million died –
Three million of them
And a little less of us.

Researchers get diplomas
And bronze plaques,
For they found the unfindable.
Celebrities get a death of their
Very own choice
And the worship of their shed skins
For ever after.

And the entranced crowds cheer
Every new head tossed
In a colosseum
(For the crowds die slowly in vain)
And every time the emperors wear new clothes
On their ever-lasting parade.

For the emperors have no-one,
But the cooks
(For let me not grow fat,
But I must have those three birds,
And one bite more, with garnish and gravy).
Cooks never die,
For they buy their lives day by day
With their art.

Ballad Which an Ageing Pop-Star Will Never Write

I was crying tonight
I was listening to some
sentimental old notes.
Oh how I hate us
who live great lives of
illusion.

Am I growing old
or am I growing wise
if I think it doesn't matter?
Am I growing weary of burnt-out
fires and lived days?

Places, faces, rooms, smiles,
eyes, tears haunting me,
carrying me away.

Yet I cry the cries of the unborn
for the sweetness of love.
And I hate notes that
devour life.

Tired and cracked in the end,
I don't care.

The Box

Once
I had some little things,
those little parts of our lives, shiny bits and pieces we like
and never know what to do with (some are useful too).

I shall have a box for all this nice junk.
A nice box, indeed.
They never do nice little boxes for our own private treasures.
I shall make one.

Look, here I have the cover of that old notebook.
I really liked it – that's why I have kept it, till now.
And here is that calendar with old maps
my uncle sent me some years ago.
I'll glue them on the other side.
It looks like a real treasure map.

I've used all my glue.
It doesn't mattter. I can use sellotape.
And on the back of the box I can put this lovely wrapping
paper.
That's what my birthday gift from my sister came out of.
I can't remember what it was, but I liked it.
That's why I kept the paper.

Oh look, some old tickets to the opera.
Yes, we went together. I really liked that girl.
They will look like some sticker-souvenirs
from journeys into romantic memory.
And this postcard from the Old Land will fit well.

Ooops, I've run out of sellotape.
I'll use this leather ribbon.

In her hair it looked like a twisted spark from a firework.
Then she forgot it and never came back.
The card will be like a lid on the treasure
secured by the Gordian knot of the ribbon.
It really does look good.

Oh, here is a dry little rosebud.
I'll staple it like a lock on the box.
Lucky me. The last staple.

What shall I put into the box?

#0084 - 111018 - C0 - 210/148/4 - PB - DID2327807